About Me

About Me

· · · · · · · · · · · · · · · · · · · ·

Contents

What can I do?

I can use my **senses** to learn about the world.

look

I can use my eyes to look.

listen

I can use my ears to listen.

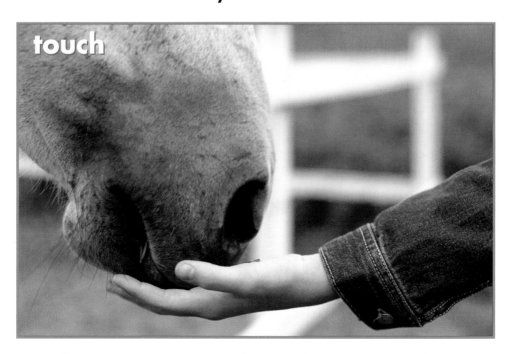

touch

I can use my hands to touch.

smell

I can use my nose to smell.

taste

I can use my tongue to taste.

I can use my arms and legs.
I can jump and run.

I can take care of myself.

I can take care of Earth.

What do I need to grow?

I **need** good food to eat.

I need water to drink.

I need air to breathe.

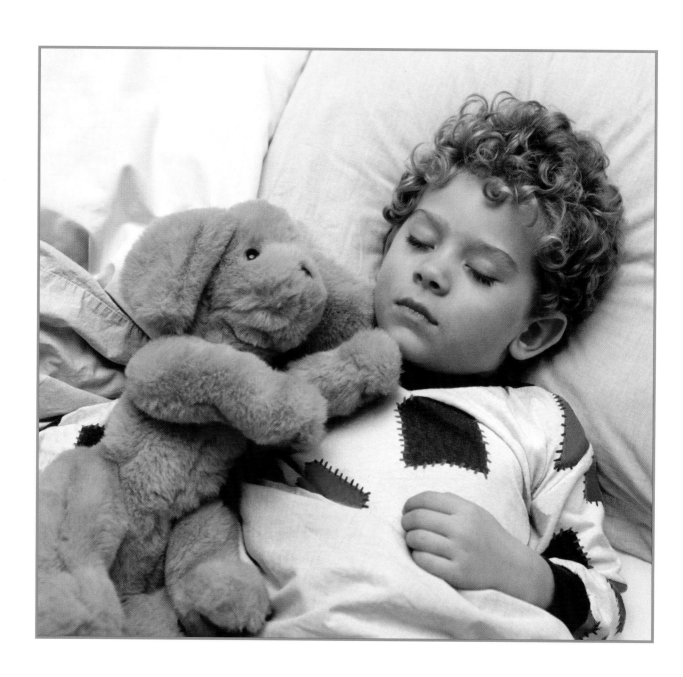

I need a good night's sleep.

I need **shelter**. I need a place to live.

How will I change?

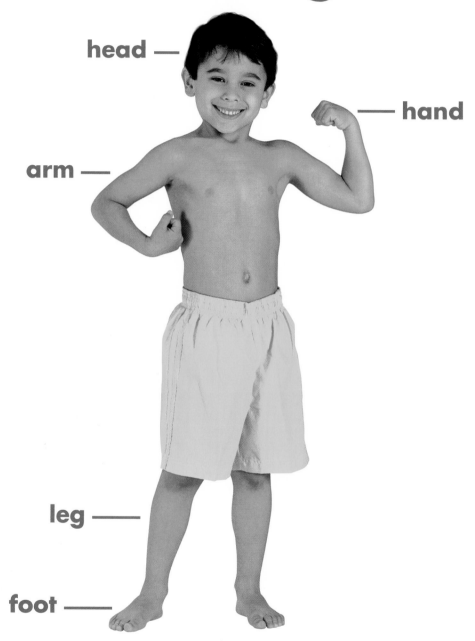

head —

— hand

arm —

leg —

foot —

I am a person.

People are **living** things.

I will get bigger.

I will **grow** and **change**.

Glossary

change to look different

grow to get bigger

living something alive that grows and changes

need must have

senses looking, listening, touching, smelling, tasting

shelter a place where we live and may be safe